# Introduc

**Q**uiet **Welsh valleys** in the sunsh floor and the slopes above, and t the whistle of a steam engine and down the line. These are sights and sou fundamental part of our holidays in Wale. the Welsh countryside than the preserved steam trains that run through it. The Welsh landscape is one which has been used for different purposes for many centuries. Although today we see mostly grazing land, slate, copper, manganese and even gold mining all have left their mark on the countryside. And the preserved railways are usually where they are precisely because of the industrial heritage of the landscape. Valleys which are quiet and rural today were bustling centres of Victorian industry 150 years ago.

We have written these walks to help walkers of all abilities, fitness levels and ages to explore the Welsh countryside further. We also wanted to help families to introduce their children to the delights of exploring the hills and valleys. Our own children have, sometimes reluctantly, joined us on these walks and almost invariably enjoyed them in the end! The walks vary in difficulty from the Llyn Stwlan and Snowdon walks which can, in inclement weather, provide a stiff test for an average walker, to those like the Montgomery Canal which are more of a relaxed stroll. But all are within the compass of a reasonably fit and willing walker.

Knowing that sometimes the promise of a walk in the hills and valleys is not sufficiently attractive to everyone we have designed these walks to start and end at a railway station on one of the preserved steam railways in North and Mid Wales so they can be combined with a ride on one of the railways. We have not, in a small book of 20 walks, tried to cover all the Great Little Trains of Wales. So this book includes walks from the Ffestiniog, Welsh Highland, Welsh Highland Heritage, Bala Lake, Fairbourne, Talyllyn, Vale of Rheidol and Welshpool & Llanfair railways. My own favourite walks are from the Talyllyn, but this is certainly influenced by my childhood riding the Talyllyn railway and exploring the Fathew and Dysinni valleys!

We have also given an alternative start point of a car park, or car parking place, so that all of these walks can just as easily be walked from a car park and not necessarily from a station.

We hope you enjoy exploring these walks as much as we have!

*For my late father, Eric, who introduced me to the delights of both walking and steam railways.*

# WALK I
# SNOWDON
# YR WYDDFA

**DESCRIPTION** No book of walks from railways in Wales is complete without a walk up Snowdon. This strenuous walk brings together two of the traditional routes up Snowdon; the Rhyd-Ddu Path and the Snowdon Ranger Path. The walk from Rhyd-Ddu Station up Snowdon and back to Snowdon Ranger Station takes 5 hours and is 7 miles long. The train back from Snowdon Ranger Station takes 15 minutes. The bus takes 5 minutes. *Check the relevant timetables before you go.*
**START** From Rhyd-Ddu Station on the Welsh Highland Railway. There is also a car park at Rhyd-Ddu Station, with public conveniences.

*The Rhyd-Ddu Path is the route of the first recorded ascent of Snowdon in 1639, by Thomas Johnson. The Snowdon Ranger Path was named after John Morton, one of Snowdonia's first guides, who opened the Snowdon Ranger Inn at the beginning of the 19th century. The path may well be the oldest route up the mountain. As always care is needed when climbing mountains, and Snowdon is no exception. Make sure you have the correct footwear, warm clothing and waterproofs, and check the weather forecast before you leave. Conditions which are mild in the valleys can be difficult on the mountains.*

**I** Walk to the end of the platform, and turn right through a metal gate across the track. As you climb the path is well marked and clear, and rises steadily between rocky outcrops, and then across open hillside.

**2** At a clear crossroads, follow the sign left to Yr Wyddfa through another gate, and the path becomes a stone built path. *The path climbs to a large cairn, with a beautiful view to the north over Llyn Ffynnon-y-gwas reservoir around which you will be walking later. Pause here for a few moments to take in the view and prepare yourself for a steeper climb ahead.* The path then climbs steeply up towards Llechog Ridge.

**3** Through a gate in a dry stone wall you climb to Llechog Ridge, which appropriately means Rocky Place. After an easy start the path rises steeply and affords magnificent views south towards Yr Aran. *The path here is exposed to winds which can be very strong.* As you climb further a fence marks the path and leads you up through a series of zigzags towards the next ridge, Bwlch Main, which means Narrow Pass. The path here is narrow and exposed to the wind. There are also a couple of sections where a little light scrambling is required. In the summer this is within the capabilities of almost all walkers. In the winter proper equipment is necessary. The path at Bwlch Main leads you up

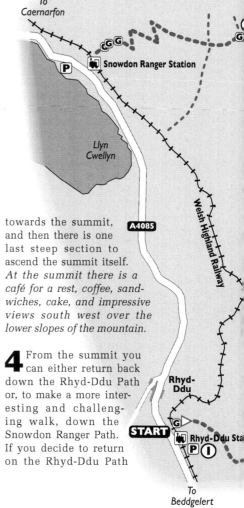

towards the summit, and then there is one last steep section to ascend the summit itself. *At the summit there is a café for a rest, coffee, sandwiches, cake, and impressive views south west over the lower slopes of the mountain.*

**4** From the summit you can either return back down the Rhyd-Ddu Path or, to make a more interesting and challenging walk, down the Snowdon Ranger Path. If you decide to return on the Rhyd-Ddu Path take care to ignore the Watkin Path which leaves our path to the left just below the summit, and also to ignore the path to the left across Clogwyn Du along Bwlch Main. To take the Snowdon Ranger Path back, follow the Snowdon Mountain Railway track for 400 yards until you see the large standing stone marking the start of the Pyg Track and Miners' Track going steeply down to the right. *At this stone, if the weather is kind, you will see amazing views to the east across Carnedd Ugain and Crib Goch and the two lakes of Glaslyn and Llyn Llydaw.*

**6** The path goes through a metal gate in a fence. Follow the path past a marker post showing the path to Llanberis and continue along the Snowdon Ranger Path as it begins to descend again through another series of gentle zigzags. At the bottom of these go through the metal gate, and then another metal gate past Llwyn Onn farmhouse and then another next to a cattle grid. Cross the Welsh Highland Railway track and turn immediately left to walk onto the platform of Snowdon Ranger Station. From this station, which is a request halt, take the train back to Rhyd-Ddu.

**5** At the standing stone bear left to keep close to the railway track and then at the next standing stone cross over the railway track and follow the Snowdon Ranger Path which is clearly marked as you lose height steadily down the mountainside. *In the distance to your left you will see Llyn Cwellyn reservoir. On a clear day you may also see the Menai Straits and Anglesey ahead to your left. To your right you will see the slate mines above Llanberis.* The path becomes steeper as you descend Clogwyn Du'r Arddu ridge. The path keeps well below the line of the ridge and is somewhat sheltered and eventually views of Llanberis itself open up to your right. For the steeper descents as you come down towards Llyn Ffynnon-y-gwas the path zigzags down the hillside. Below Llyn Ffynnon-y-gwas the path flattens out and the descent becomes gentle.

Signal the train driver clearly to request him to halt. If there is no train available, follow the path down to the main road at the Snowdon Ranger Youth Hostel and turn right to walk a few yards to the bus stop where you can take the Snowdon Sherpa bus service back to Rhyd-Ddu.

## WALK 2

# BEDDGELERT TO CWM BYCHAN & LLYN DINAS

**DESCRIPTION** A moderate and delightful walk from Beddgelert Station on the Welsh Highland Railway up Cwm Bychan to Llyn Dinas with unforgettable views to the Snowdon massif and across Llyn Dinas. 3½ hours, 4¾ miles. This walk can be shortened to a ½ hour walk along the river and back.

**START** From Beddgelert Station on the Welsh Highland Railway.

**1** Leave the station and bear right through the car park to the main road (A498), and turn left. Just before the road bridge turn right at the signpost marked Gelert's Grave. You will pass public conveniences before crossing the footbridge ahead of you. If you have time you can turn right just before the footbridge and walk the 400 yards to Gelert's Grave which lies on the path in the shade of two trees. *According to legend Gelert was the faithful hound of Prince Llewelyn the great in the 13th century which is said to have saved Prince Llewelyn's baby son from an attack by a mighty wolf. Gelert's Grave is in the grounds of a former Augustinian Priory which was based around St Mary's Church which itself had its origins in a 6th century Celtic Christian community established at Beddgelert.*

**2** Cross the footbridge over Afon Glaslyn and turn right on a concrete path next to the river. Pass through two metal gates, and as you walk the valley begins to close in with the majestic cliffs of Craig y Llan rising to your left. You arrive at a footbridge crossing back across the river. If you have time for a short stroll only, cross the bridge and turn right on the far bank of the river to return to the first bridge and retrace your steps to the car park (total ½ hour, 1¼ miles).

**3** If you are continuing on for the longer walk, ignore the footbridge, cross over the Welsh Highland Railway line and turn left to keep the river on your right and the railway on your left. The path now becomes a very well-constructed and maintained rock path. At times the path clings to the edge of the rocks a few feet above the water. In wet weather the path can be slippery.

**4** At Pont Aberglaslyn turn left up a few rock steps and then continue through a mature deciduous wood, next to a fence. The fence falls away to your right but continue straight ahead on the path. Go through a wooden gate and continue through the woodland. At a signpost follow the path right towards a car park, and before the car park bear left over a stone stile and through the tunnel under the Welsh Highland Railway to a picnic area. Beyond the picnic area bear left on the well-marked path up the hillside, ignoring the path sharp left which takes you back to the railway. Pass through a wooden gate – *and pause to look behind you at the views over Nantmor and the Afon Glaswyn behind you.* The path climbs next to a stream and on a hot day you can rest for a while to cool your feet in the stream. You are now climbing gently and steadily up into Cwm Bychan and you can see the valley begin to open up ahead of you. *You may hear and see cuckoos on a spring day in the peaceful valley.* The path crosses the stream across some stepping stones and then goes through a stone wall to your right. *As you climb the valley you see the well-preserved remains of a cable car system which used to take copper ore down to the Welsh Highland Railway at Nantmor, a reminder of the industrial heritage in what are now very peaceful valleys.*

**5** Just beyond the final cable car support, and a large heap of tailings to the left, the path divides. Take the right hand fork going straight ahead up the valley. Continue to climb as the valley narrows around you. At the top of the pass there is a ladder stile. Cross the stile to a large rock – *where you can rest and you are rewarded with unforgettable views north east over Llyn Dinas, and north over Yr Aran in the foreground and Snowdon*

*(Yr Wyddfa) and Yr Lliwedd in the middle distance. Bear left 100 yards to a signpost.*

**6** At the signpost turn right on the path down towards Llyn Dinas. Continue on the path as the valley opens out ahead of you. The path bears left away from the stream and descends more steeply towards Llyn Dinas ahead of you, offering more stunning views across the lake past Yr Aran and towards Snowdon again.

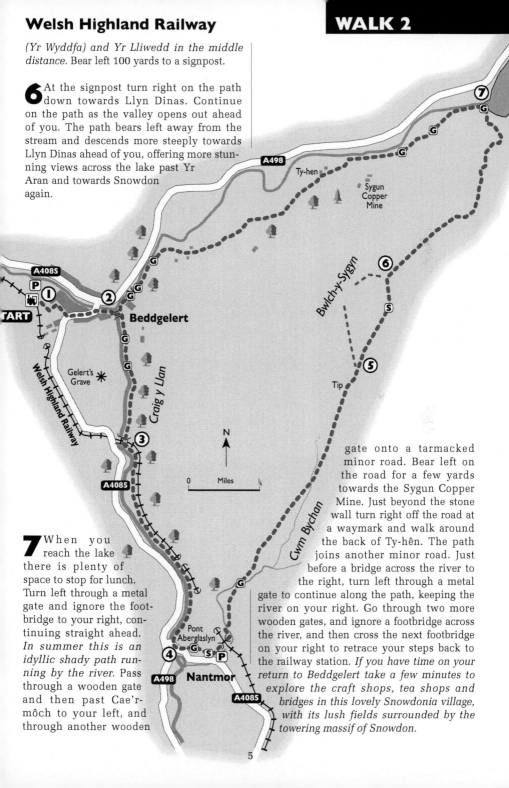

**7** When you reach the lake there is plenty of space to stop for lunch. Turn left through a metal gate and ignore the footbridge to your right, continuing straight ahead. *In summer this is an idyllic shady path running by the river.* Pass through a wooden gate and then past Cae'r-môch to your left, and through another wooden gate onto a tarmacked minor road. Bear left on the road for a few yards towards the Sygun Copper Mine. Just beyond the stone wall turn right off the road at a waymark and walk around the back of Ty-hên. The path joins another minor road. Just before a bridge across the river to the right, turn left through a metal gate to continue along the path, keeping the river on your right. Go through two more wooden gates, and ignore a footbridge across the river, and then cross the next footbridge on your right to retrace your steps back to the railway station. *If you have time on your return to Beddgelert take a few minutes to explore the craft shops, tea shops and bridges in this lovely Snowdonia village, with its lush fields surrounded by the towering massif of Snowdon.*

# THE PORTMEIRION HEADLAND

**DESCRIPTION** An easy walk through the town Porthmadog, across the causeway and around the Portmeirion headland. 3½ miles, 2½ hours round trip.

**START** From the Welsh Highland Heritage Railway station at Porthmadog.

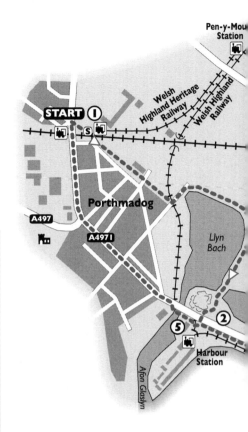

**1** Walk along the platform towards the town, and at the end of the platform take the stile on your left to cross over the railway. *This is the main line railway so take care to stop, look and listen for trains. The Welsh Highland (Heritage) Railway had a short operating history, opening in 1922 and closing in 1937.* Across the railway bear left and follow the path on the bank above the road. Ignore the footpath sign to the left and cross over a small minor road onto a tarmac road directly ahead and at the next crossroads turn left crossing over the narrow gauge railway line. Just across the bridge bear right at the footpath sign and follow the embankment around the tidal enclosure of Llyn Bach. *Very quickly you are out of the town and lovely vistas towards the Snowdon range to your left open up.* Walk across the concrete bridge over the sluice gates and follow the minor road around to meet the main A487

**2** Cross the A487 taking care of traffic and walk into Ffestiniog Railway Harbour Station. Bear left and follow the path along the causeway next to the Ffestiniog Railway line, towards Boston Lodge a mile ahead of you. *Boston Lodge is where the Ffestiniog Railway still carries out maintenance on its rolling stock. As you cross the causeway you see the most wonderful views to your left up across the marshes towards the Snowdon massif and to your right across the sandy marsh lands towards the bay and open sea. Ahead of you is the green and wooded headland of Portmeirion, with the vil-lage on the far side. Behind you are views of Porthmadog, with Moel y gest and its disused quarries rising above the town. On a cold winters afternoon this causeway can be very blustery. In the marshes to the left and right you will see many gulls and waders including curlews and terns.* As you reach the end of the causeway go down the steps as signposted and carefully cross the road to the path on the other side and continue right along the cycle track. After the cycle track re-joins the main road you will see a footpath signpost across the road. Cross the road again carefully and follow the path up to Boston Lodge halt. Cross the Ffestiniog line and proceed to a wooden gate at the sign marked Public Footpath. Proceed through the gate and bear right on a gently rising path up the hillside, through deciduous woods. You very quickly leave the bustle of the road and the station behind you.

**3** At a fork in the path with a well hidden sign post bear right, and you will begin to see views over the causeway and Porthmadog become visible between the trees to your right. Pass through a wooden gate and continue up the grassy path. As the

487

Main Line Railway - Pwllheli to Machynlleth

path emerges from the woods it becomes a little overgrown, *but provides great autumn blackberrying opportunities and views open up between the trees out to sea and across the Llyn peninsula.* Pass through a wooden gate into a beautiful pastured valley – with views west over the sea and east towards

**4** Follow the bridle path left through the old farm buildings. Cross another cattle grid and views over the marshes open up to your left. Just after Plas Penrhyn take the path which turns sharp left, signposted Bron Madog. Go through the metal gate by the house and follow the path across the field to the track. Turn left on the track and after 100 yards turn right on to a path between two dry stone walls down the hillside to Boston Lodge Halt. From here retrace your steps back across to the causeway and to Porthmadog.

**5** An alternative route back to your start point is to walk through Porthmadog instead of around Llyn Bach. As you leave the Ffestiniog Railway station turn left along the main road through

The Cob

Ffestiniog Railway

A4971

Plas Penrhyn

N

Boston Lodge Station
Railway Works

G ③

④

0   Miles   ¼

G

G

Penrhos isaf

G

the mountains. Bear right across the field heading for a wooden gate with a very old way mark sign. Continue through the wooden gate, and turn immediately left following the fence. Go through the farmyard of Penrhyn Isaf on your right, and return to the track, keeping the fence on your left. Cross the cattle grid and continue to follow the track to a crossroads of paths in the yard of a ruined farm

Porthmadog (A497). At the roundabout bear right, cross the main line railway, and arrive back at the Welsh Highland Railway. *There are plenty of bakeries and sandwich shops along the main road, and even a restaurant at the Welsh Highland Heritage Railway serving tasty roast lunches.*

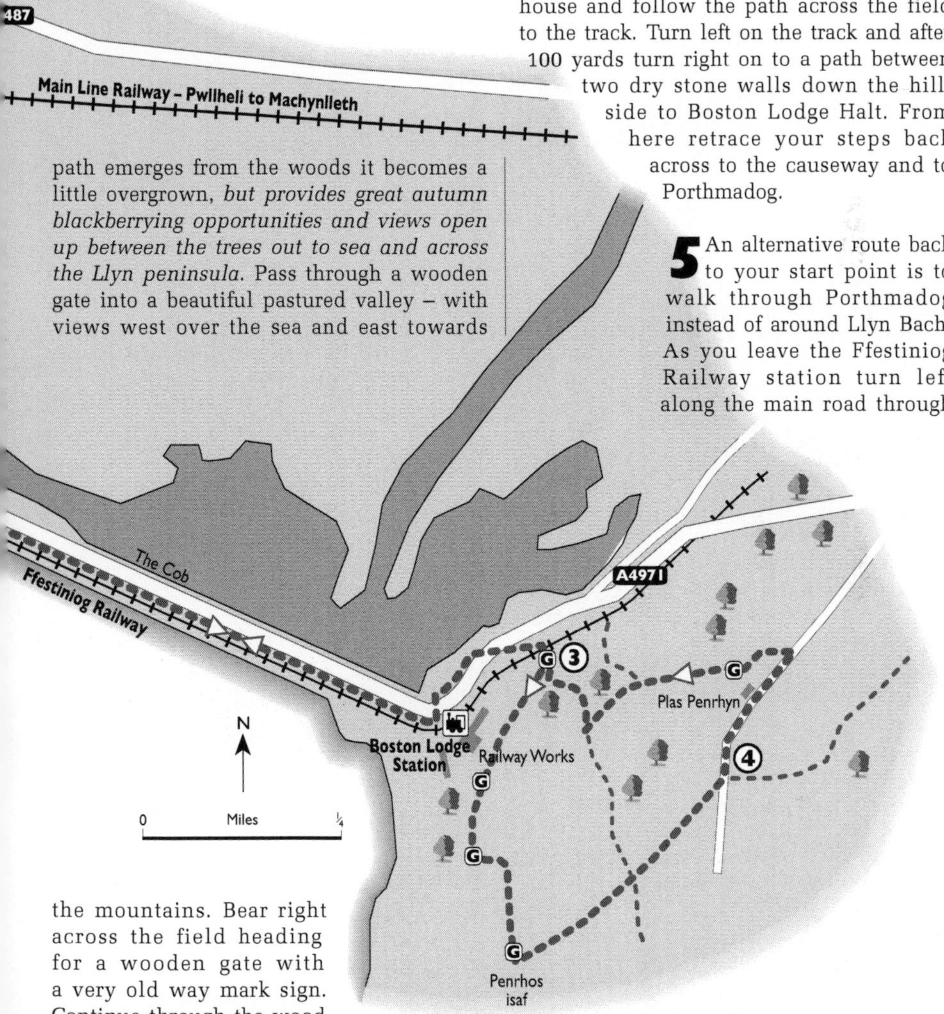

# DDUALT STATION & GOLYGFAN VIEWPOINT

**DESCRIPTION** An easy walk with gentle climbs from Tanygrisiau Station on the Ffestiniog Railway, around Tanygrisiau Reservoir, and along to Dduallt Station and the Golygfan viewpoint over the Vale of Ffestiniog, and back. 2¾ hours, 3½ miles.

**START** From Tanygrisiau Station on the Ffestiniog Railway. From the station look out across the reservoir. You will be walking around the eastern side of the reservoir and over the hill at the far end, then back around the western side. An alternative starting point is the public car park 200 yards south and east down the minor road which serves Tanygrisiau Station.

**I** From Tanygrisiau Station car park turn right onto the minor road and walk past the Lakeside Café on your right. As the road bends sharply to the right, you will see a green footpath sign to your left. Follow this through a metal gate and up a tarmacked track. Cross over the Ffestiniog Railway, checking carefully for trains and continue up the track until you see another green footpath sign to your left. Follow the path left as it leaves the tarmac track and descends back down to the reservoir, over a wooden footbridge and stile, crossing back over the Ffestiniog Railway and around the back of the Ffestiniog Power Station. *Tan-y-grisiau Reservoir is a man-made reservoir, constructed to serve the Ffestiniog Power Station, built in 1963. The Power Station can supply the electricity requirements of the whole of North Wales.* Green waymarks lead you back to the edge of the reservoir.

**2** After 50 yards or so a waymark takes you back up towards the Ffestiniog Railway again. Cross over the railway through a pair of metal gates and turn immediately left as the path climbs gently up, with the railway on your left. Follow the path past some concrete foundations on your right, then look for a waymark sign embedded in an old oak tree above you to your right. Follow the path up and under a stone bridge and then across a wooden footbridge. Beyond the bridge, at a yellow waymark, the path crosses through a stone wall and descends the hillside to a pair of ladder stiles to cross the railway. Cross the railway, checking for trains as usual, and go straight ahead following the path to a grassy track 50 yards up the hill side.

**3** Turn right on the grassy track and follow it up the gentle hill at the end of the reservoir. The Ffestiniog Railway to your right goes into a small cutting, and then into a tunnel through the hill. As you come over the top of the hill you will see the Ffestiniog line exit the tunnel. *This is a lovely sight when a steam engine exits the tunnel. Ahead of you lies the Vale of Ffestiniog.* Follow the path as it snakes along, just to the left of the railway line. An old dismantled narrow gauge line appears to your left and joins your path. *As it joins you will just make out in the distance ahead of you the building housing the disused reactors of the Trawsfynydd Magnox Power Station.* As you enter a small wood the path bears left away from the disused railway line at a yellow marker post. After 50 yards another marker post leads you up and into an oak wood. This path takes you along to the left of the old railway line, through a metal kissing gate, and rejoins the Ffestiniog Railway.

**4** Cross the line carefully to arrive at Dduallt Station. At the far end of the station there is a ladder stile to the left. Cross the stile to climb up to the Golygfan viewpoint – *from where on a clear day you will see the Vale of Ffestiniog, Trawsfynydd and Blaenau Ffestiniog visible up the valley behind you with Manod Bach and Manod Mawr towering over Blaenau Ffestiniog. You will also see the loop in the Ffestiniog Railway where the railway gains height for its climb up to Tanygrisiau and Blaenau Ffestiniog itself.* From the viewing point retrace your steps to Dduallt Station, and then back to Tanygrisiau Reservoir.

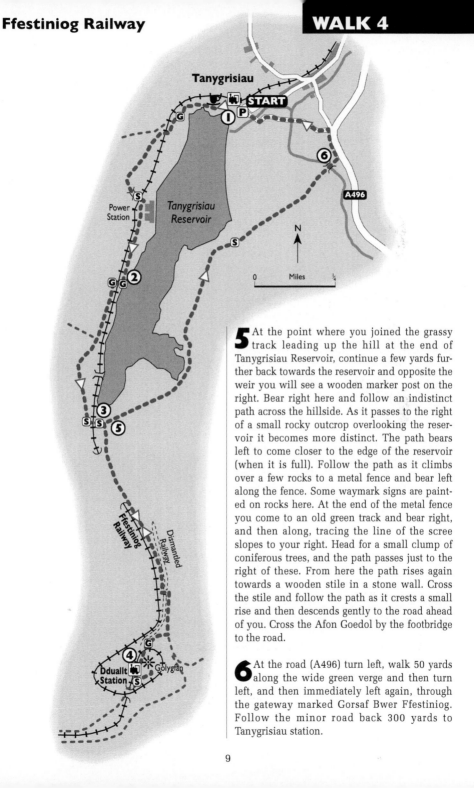

**Tanygrisiau**

**START**

Tanygrisiau Reservoir

Power Station

N

0      Miles      ¼

A496

Ffestiniog Railway

Dismantled Railway

Dduallt Station

Golygfan

**5** At the point where you joined the grassy track leading up the hill at the end of Tanygrisiau Reservoir, continue a few yards further back towards the reservoir and opposite the weir you will see a wooden marker post on the right. Bear right here and follow an indistinct path across the hillside. As it passes to the right of a small rocky outcrop overlooking the reservoir it becomes more distinct. The path bears left to come closer to the edge of the reservoir (when it is full). Follow the path as it climbs over a few rocks to a metal fence and bear left along the fence. Some waymark signs are painted on rocks here. At the end of the metal fence you come to an old green track and bear right, and then along, tracing the line of the scree slopes to your right. Head for a small clump of coniferous trees, and the path passes just to the right of these. From here the path rises again towards a wooden stile in a stone wall. Cross the stile and follow the path as it crests a small rise and then descends gently to the road ahead of you. Cross the Afon Goedol by the footbridge to the road.

**6** At the road (A496) turn left, walk 50 yards along the wide green verge and then turn left, and then immediately left again, through the gateway marked Gorsaf Bwer Ffestiniog. Follow the minor road back 300 yards to Tanygrisiau station.

# LLYN STWLAN

**DESCRIPTION** A strenuous walk from Tanygrisiau station on the Ffestiniog Railway up to Llyn Stwlan, around the cwm and back to Tanygrisiau station. Stunning views make the walk well worthwhile. The walk includes some parts where the footpath is indistinct and difficult to find. For experienced walkers only, and not recommended for children. 4 hours, 5 miles.
**START** From Tanygrisiau Station on the Ffestiniog Railway. An alternative starting point is the public car park 200 yards south and east down the minor road which serves Tanygrisiau Station.

**1** Turn right out of Tanygrisiau station car park and head past the cafe on your right. Follow the road as it turns sharp right back on itself and crosses the Ffestiniog line (take care for trains!).

**2** Look out for the weir to the right, and then do not cross the bridge on the right, but leave the road and head straight on to the metal gate with a kissing gate to the left. Go through the kissing gate and continue up the metalled track (which is the access road for infrequent traffic to Llyn Stwlan). *To your right you will see a small waterfall, and then you will pass the old Wrysgan quarry incline to your right. The last part of the incline is a tunnel through the rock!* Continue up the metalled track. This is a long steady climb. *Look out for the tremendous views as they develop across Tanygrisiau reservoir, and back toward Tanygrisiau, Blaenau Ffestiniog, over the Trawsfynydd power station, and even as far as Cadair Idris on clear days.*

**3** As the reservoir retaining wall comes into view above you, take a left at the waymark sign off the metalled track on to a path. Cross over a small stream past some ruined buildings, and cross the ladder stile ahead of you. Just after the ladder stile turn right on the built up grassy path for 50 yards. Then head straight up towards the reservoir wall, next to the remains of an old wall,

keeping close to the fence on your right. Just before the reservoir wall there is a waymark pointing left. Follow the arrow left steeply up between two small outcrops. At the top of the short climb you will see another waymark sign ahead of you – *but take a few minutes here to look back at Blaenau Ffestiniog and the view south.* (At the waymark take a short detour to your right, up the stone steps and along the reservoir wall.) From the way-

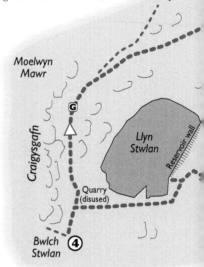

mark follow the indistinct path which goes straight ahead, to the corner of the low dam wall and take the stone steps to the right up and round the edge of the reservoir. From here follow the indistinct path along the side of the reservoir, heading just to the left of an old disused mine building ahead of you. There is another short steep climb up to meet the path you will take later, and then on a few yards left up to the col – *which gives you superb views over the Llyn Peninsula and the Snowdon range.*

**4** Do not continue over the col, but return down to where you met the path and turn left to skirt around the back wall of the cwm, with Craigysgafn towering above you to your left. (If you did not go the last few yards up to the col then you would turn right when you meet the path.) *You will see beautiful views over Llyn Stwlan to your right.* The path is clear, but gradually becomes

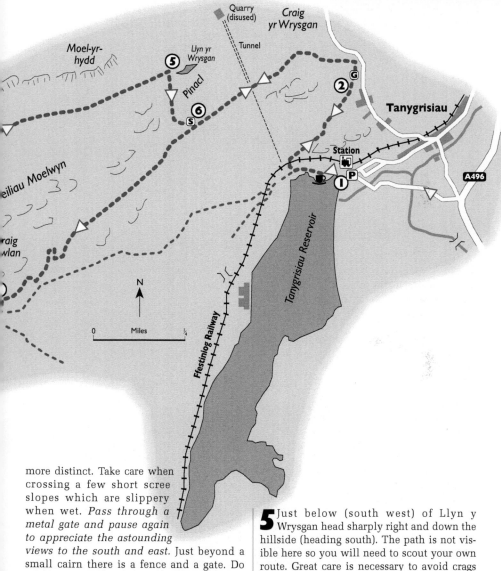

more distinct. Take care when crossing a few short scree slopes which are slippery when wet. *Pass through a metal gate and pause again to appreciate the astounding views to the south and east.* Just beyond a small cairn there is a fence and a gate. Do not go through the gate, but turn right to follow the path downhill. There are other paths marked on the maps for the area, but which are not clearly visible on the ground. Follow this path down and around the southern slopes of Moel-yr-hydd. Continue to follow the very indistinct path to the east until you get close to the very small lake Llyn y Wrysgan, clearly visible ahead.

**5** Just below (south west) of Llyn y Wrysgan head sharply right and down the hillside (heading south). The path is not visible here so you will need to scout your own route. Great care is necessary to avoid crags and steep falls, and in the wet it is also very slippery.

**6** Cross back onto the metalled track across the ladder stile at the bottom of the slope, and follow the metalled track left, back down to the metal gate and kissing gate. Retrace your steps back the last ½ mile to Tanygrisiau station.

11

## WALK 6

# THE VALE OF FFESTINIOG & RHYD Y SARN

**DESCRIPTION** A moderate walk from Dduallt Station towards Tan-y-bwlch, and back up the Vale of Ffestiniog including some lovely upland pasture, mature deciduous and pine woods, and views over the Vale of Ffestiniog. 3½ hours, 5½ miles.

**START** From Dduallt Station on the Ffestiniog Railway. An alternative start point is the lay-by at Rhyd-y-sarn (see 6 below).

**I** Head towards the south end of the station and, before you start the walk, take the time to walk up to the Golygfan viewpoint over the ladder stile to the left. *At the viewpoint stands a map table and on a clear day you will be able to identify the Vale of Ffestiniog, Trawsfynydd and Blaenau Ffestiniog visible up the valley behind you with Manod Bach and Manod Mawr above.* Return to Dduallt Station to start the walk from the ladder stile on the right signposted to Tan-y-bwlch Station, Oakley Arms and Plas y Dduallt. Cross the ladder stile, and turn left to pass under the railway bridge and then follow the path right. *You walk across gentle upland pasture and views over the Vale of Ffestinog open up as you rejoin the railway on the left.* Cross the railway over the ladder stile, and follow the path right down to the hamlet of Dduallt and a metalled track with a house on the corner, with an interesting fence with upside down pencils as fence posts opposite!

**2** Follow the green footpath sign pointing right just beyond the house, climbing up the hillside, and then through a wooden kissing gate into Coedydd Maentwrog. Climb gently up through a mature deciduous wood to the cottage of Coed-y-bleiddiau – *where it is said that the last wild wolf in Wales was killed. This is commemorated by a living willow sculpture opposite the cottage.* The

path crosses a footbridge below the railway line. Ignore the path heading steeply down the valley to the left and continue straight on. At an information board for Coedydd Maentwrog keep left, heading for a waymark sign and wooden gate leading into the mature pine forest. After 200 yards ignore the path leaving to the left and carry straight on. The path becomes a track and curves right over a small stream, and then past a cattle grid. Follow the track along and down to meet the B4410 at Llyn Mair, where you will find a picnic spot 200 yards along the road to the right.

**3** If you are not picnicking, turn left on the road heading south. *Take care on the road as although it is quiet there is no footpath, but the verges are easily wide enough to walk along.* As the road heads steeply downhill and left, look for a green footpath sign on the left. Follow the waymarked track left back into Coedydd Maentwrog and at the house Ty Coch follow the waymarked path left. Just above the house take the right fork stepping over a large fallen tree, then cross a small footbridge. The path climbs back up the hillside through mature deciduous woodland, then descends increasingly steeply towards the road. Turn right at a waymarked path down to a wooden gate which leads you to a minor road.

**4** Turn left, and past the tiny hamlet of Bronturnor with the Afon Dwyryd meandering quietly to your right. Continue along this road for 2 miles and follow it over the old Pont-Dol-y-moch bridge over the Afon Dwyryd. The minor road bears left to join the A496.

**5** Turn right on the A496 for 25 yards, and then left on the B4391. After 25 yards follow the green footpath sign to the right, uphill into mature deciduous woods. Cross a ladder stile and continue out of the woods, keeping the dry stone wall on your left. As

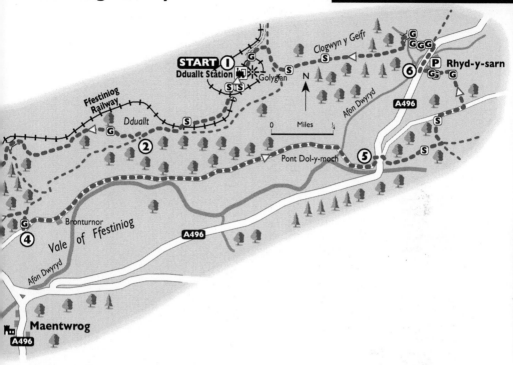

the wall turns sharp left follow the wall left across the hillside keeping the wall on your left. At the B4391 cross the stile and turn right on the road for 200 yards and then left at a green footpath sign downhill. The dry stone wall on your left has fallen down in places and the path is quite overgrown. At the bottom of the path go through a metal kissing gate and turn left at a waymark on an electricity pole. Go through another metal gate and turn almost immediately right through another, well-hidden, metal gate between two dry stone walls.

**6** Turn right and walk along the A496 for 100 yards to a lay-by on the right hand side of the road at Rhyd-y-sarn. This is an alternative start point for the walk. Turn left on a track immediately beyond (northeast of) the bridge and through a metal gate. Go past the house on the left and through another metal gate, and the track becomes a path. At the Afon Goedol follow the green footpath sign through the metal gate into Coed Cwmerau National Nature Reserve

and up next to the river. Turn left across the footbridge, guarded by a small wooden gate, over a deep dark pool in the river, an oasis between the rapids above and below the pool. The short climb up beyond the river gives you lovely views over Afon Goedol and over the Vale of Ffestiniog. As you climb up the valley you leave the Nature Reserve and enter a mature pine forest. Climb up through the pine forest, and at a waymark post the path appears to divide. Take the right hand path and the bulk of Clogwyn y Deifr towers above you to your right. Cross a ladder stile to exit the wood and keep close to the dry stone wall on your right as you cross a small patch of moorland. Cross another ladder stile on your right to cross over the wall and head left on the path as it climbs further up the valley and then bear right on a rough track. As you crest the hill into a quiet valley the track appears to divide. Take the left fork and after 100 yards turn left at a well-hidden waymark post to return through a metal gate to Dduallt Station.

# ABOVE BALA LAKE

**DESCRIPTION** A moderate short walk from the Bala Lake Railway at the northern end of Bala Lake (Llyn Tegid) into the hills, with stunning views over the lake and surroundings. 2½ miles, 1½ hours round trip.

**START** At Bala Lake Station, on the Bala Lake Railway, outside Bala. (An alternative starting point is the car park at the Tourist Information Centre at Bala. From the back of the Tourist Information Centre walk left on the tarmac path running along the side of the lake, keeping the lake on your right. Bear right at the minor road, bear right onto B4391 across the road bridge, and then bear right again over another small old bridge to Bala Lake Station.)

**1** From the railway station, cross the footbridge heading away from the lake. Go through the black kissing gate and bear right across the field to the ladder stile, then cross the next field to the wooden stile in the right hand corner. Cross the stile and turn right on the gravelled track. Cross the stile to the right of the metal gate and follow the track through the car park and then through the Bala Lake Hotel. *The Hotel is now privately owned but the path is still open for public access.* Just beyond the cattle grid bear left up the hillside following the green footpath sign, entering some attractive deciduous woodland. Cross the next wooden stile, pausing to take in the view to your right across the lake and back towards the town of Bala behind you, and then take the path going straight on.

**2** The path takes you round the back of Graienyn, and rises up the hillside passing some oaks and enters deciduous woodland of sycamore and ash. At a waymark sign follow the path right and a little downwards to cross over the stream next to Ffridd Goed, then head back up the hillside, bearing right to keep the fence on your right. Cross another stile at a waymark and follow the path left up the hillside. *As you climb, take time to admire the unfolding views of Bala Lake to your right and behind. The countryside opens out as you cross the moorland continuing gently up hill.* Look out for the waymark sign ahead of you, on a metalled track.

**3** Turn left on the track, admiring the end-to-end views along Bala Lake and across to Moel y Garnedd opposite, and cross a cattle grid. After the cattle grid ignore the stony track to your left and continue to bear right up the tarmac road and through a metal gate. Follow the track through young coniferous forests on your right and mixed forests on your left.

**4** Just before Cefn-ddwygraig turn left down the hillside. Cross a ladder stile and head diagonally left up the hill side ahead of you ignoring the path that goes sharply left. Over the crest of the hill head down to a ladder stile and waymark in the fence ahead of you. Cross the ladder stile and head across the next field keeping close to the fence on your left. Cross the next stile and head diagonally right across the next field to the next stile ahead of you, and you see the town of Bala spread out below you. Cross the next stile and head steeply down the field to a waymark in the right hand corner ahead of you. Bear right following the waymark towards a coniferous forest, and cross a stile to enter the woods. Follow the path downhill through the forest and when it crosses the edge of a stony forestry track do not follow the forestry track but continue bearing right at the green footpath signpost.

**5** At the tarmac road at the bottom turn sharply left, and where the track divides take the right hand fork. At the waymark sign pointing right, cross the stile and retrace your steps to Bala Lake Station.

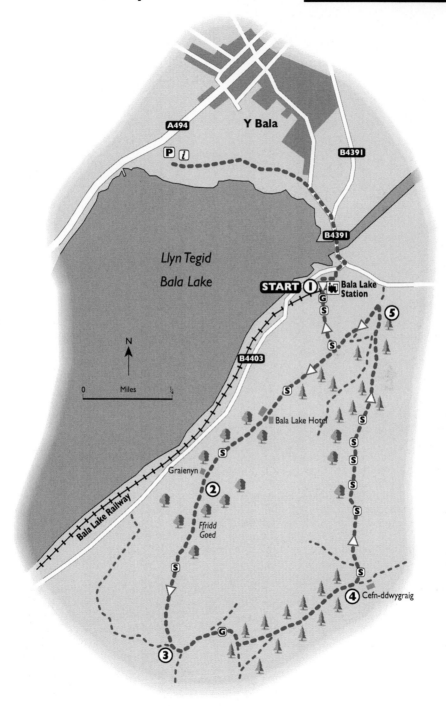

Y Bala

A494

P i

B4391

B4391

Llyn Tegid
Bala Lake

START 1 Bala Lake
Station

G

S

N

0 Miles ¼

B4403

S

S

S

Bala Lake Hotel

S

5

S

S

S

S

S

Graienyn

S

2

Ffridd
Goed

Bala Lake Railway

S

S

4 Cefn-ddwygraig

S

3

G

## WALK 8

# HILLS & FORESTS ABOVE BALA LAKE

**DESCRIPTION** A moderate walk from the Bala Lake Railway with great views over Bala Lake (Llyn Tegid), and a mix of moorland, and deciduous and coniferous woodland. 4¼ hours, 6 miles.

**START** At Bala Lake Station outside Bala. (An alternative starting point is the car park at the Tourist Information Centre at Bala. From the back of the Tourist Information Centre walk left on the path running alongside the lake. Bear right at the minor road, right again onto B4391 across the road bridge, and then again over a small old bridge to Bala Lake Station.)

**1** From the railway station, cross the footbridge heading away from the lake. Go through the black kissing gate, bear right across the field to the ladder stile, and cross the next field to the wooden stile in the right hand corner. Turn right on the gravelled track through the car park and through the Bala Lake Hotel. The Hotel is now privately owned but the path is still open for public access.

**2** Just beyond the cattle grid bear left up the hillside following the green footpath sign, entering deciduous woodland. Cross the next wooden stile and take the path round the back of Graienyn, then up the hillside past some oaks and into deciduous woodland of sycamore and ash. At a waymark sign the path goes right and down to cross over the stream next to Ffridd Goed, then back up the hillside, bearing right to keep the fence on the right. Cross another stile at a waymark and follow the path left up the hillside. *As you climb, take time to admire the unfolding views of Bala Lake to your right and behind.* Look out for a waymark sign ahead of you on a metalled road.

**3** Turn left on the road for 20 yards, then at the footpath and bridlepath sign turn right through a metal gate and up the hillside. At a waymark cross the stile to your right, and after 100 yards turn left on a path heading up the hillside. A fence comes in from the left and the path runs next to the fence as it climbs over the crest of the hill. The path continues climbing with small rocky outcrops to the right. As you crest the rises look back and on a still day the lake lies like a mirror below you. *As you continue to climb views open up ahead of you across the moors to the south of Bala Lake.* As the path comes close to the fence on the left, ignore the waymarked gate and follow the path rising gently up the hillside, following a small gully. As the path curves to the left go through a gate on the right, cross the stream and bear right up the bank towards a waymark. Bear right around the hillside following a series of faded waymarks, heading towards a forest of conifer trees. Ignore the waymarked path to the right 300 yards before the forest.

**4** Cross a small stream, go through a metal gate, and enter the forest of impressive mature conifers. After a few hundred yards follow the path out of the forest and across the hillside. The forest was felled some time ago leaving bleached white trunks, surrounded by grasses and wild flowers. Continue to follow the path past a waymark and then bearing left across and up the hillside.

**5** At the next waymark which is at a gap in an old tumbledown dry stone wall, do not go through the dry stone wall but climb left up the hillside towards a waymark. Follow the path right, and at a waymark at an old wire fence enter the conifer forest. The path rises more steeply and the forest becomes gloomy. You will see a waymark, in a clearing in the forest with a profusion of blueberry bushes, where a path comes in from the right. Turn left and the path becomes an open lane in the forest. At another waymark ignore the path to the right and continue to follow the path through the trees.

# Bala Lake Railway

**6** Cross the ladder stile to exit the forest and head straight across the moorland. *There are a few hillocks here with superb panoramic views at which to eat a late lunch.* As you crest a couple of small rises the views begin to open up north towards Carneddd y Filiau. As you crest another small rise you will see a ladder stile with a waymark ahead of you. Cross the stile and gradually descend towards Bala Lake. After 100 yards the path leaves the fence on the left and heads diagonally across the hillside to the right. The path is somewhat indistinct but curves away from the fence. Follow it to the right around the hillside and you will see another ladder stile ahead of you to the left. Cross the ladder stile and bear right around the hillock ahead of you. The path forms a clear indentation in the field as it curves around the hillock and then heads north towards the centre of Bala Lake. As you cross the field you will see a white house a mile and a half away to your right, which you will be heading towards later. *As you cross the field magnificent views over Bala Lake open up beneath you.* The path veers right and you will see a ladder stile behind a hillock ahead of you. Cross the ladder stile and bear left across the field towards the bottom left hand corner. Ignore the stile to your left and look for the ladder stile directly ahead to enter a young conifer plantation. In the plantation turn immediately left on a forestry track, then fork right on to a path at the first waymark post. Turn right on a metalled forestry road and continue through the plantation.

**7** Look for a waymark sign on the right just before Cefddwygraig and turn left to a wooden ladder stile. Then take the left path which starts close to the fence but soon leaves the fence to head right diagonally across to another ladder stile. Cross the ladder stile and head straight up the track ahead of you between the clumps of gorse. Crest the hillock and go left and downhill towards Wennallt Bryniau Bach and the Lake. Cross another ladder stile and skirt the front of the farmhouse following the waymarks through a small clump of trees to cross another ladder stile and turn right on the gravelled road. Go through a metal gate and then look for the waymark on the left. Cross the stile and head straight down the field, keeping close to the fence on the left at first, and then following the path right across the field. To the left of the house ahead enter a beautiful mixed bluebell wood, and follow the path steeply

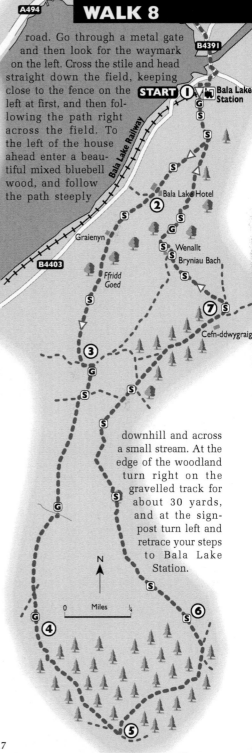

downhill and across a small stream. At the edge of the woodland turn right on the gravelled track for about 30 yards, and at the signpost turn left and retrace your steps to Bala Lake Station.

17

# WALK 9

# CEFN GWYN FROM LLANGOWER HALT

**DESCRIPTION** A moderate walk from Llangower Halt on the Bala Lake Railway up Glyn Gower and across Cefn Gwyn and back to the railway, affording pretty scenery and lovely views over Bala Lake. 3 hours, 3½ miles.

**START** From Llangower Halt on the Bala Lake Railway. The car park at Llangower Halt is an alternative start point for the walk. There are Public Conveniences in the car park.

**1** Cross the line away from the lake and head right across the car park and turn left on the B4403. Opposite the pretty church (no longer in use) by the lake turn sharp right up a minor metalled road. After a quarter of a mile the road bends to the right. At this point go straight ahead through a metal gate at a green footpath sign and follow the green path up the hillside. The path climbs the hillside with the stream forming a little gulley to the left, framed by old oak trees. *Behind you views of Bala Lake open up.*

**2** At a wooden footpath sign by an old oak tree next to a fence turn left turn down and across a wooden bridge with a wooden gate at each end. Across the bridge climb out of the gulley and cross the field directly ahead of you past a waymark to a wooden stile. Cross the stile and bear left across the field down the hill towards Ty-cerig farm, past the waymark post and a footpath sign in the field, and through a metal gate. Turn immediately right across a wooden stile and a small footbridge to another wooden stile. Cross the stile and follow the path on the left hand side of the field to a gate and another stile. Cross the stile and follow the green path as it descends gently across the hillside through an avenue of trees to another wooden stile to a stony track.

**3** Take the right hand fork as the track climbs gently up the side of the valley, through coniferous woodland. Continue up the track and you will just make out below you to your left Tyn-y-cefn farm just visible through the trees. Just past the farm, as the track crests a small rise, you will see a footpath (there is no footpath sign) going steeply up into the forest on your right. Take this path into the woods and climb up the hillside through the woods. *As you go deeper into the woods you will feel the unique stillness and calm of the woods.* The path winds through young saplings which are gradually encroaching on the path. *On a sunny day the sunlight creates beautiful patterns through the woods on the path.* As the path flattens out close to the top of the hill look to the right and you will see that a row of trees has been felled to create a path branching off up the hill. Follow this path steeply up to a waymark and a broken stile over the fence. Cross the stile and walk diagonally left over the hill, heading for the continuation of the pine forest to your left. *The path should lead back into the forest to cut the corner of the forest, but is no longer distinguishable.* When you reach the forest again follow the line of the fence right, to the corner of the forest. At the corner turn left to continue following the edge of the forest, crossing a fence which comes out from the corner of the forest as you do so. Continue to keep the forest on your left and just after the next fence you will see a waymark and a stile where the path exits the forest. From here bear diagonally right across the boggy and damp moorland, aiming to pass just to the right of the second summit of Cefn Gwyn. *As you cross the hill amazing views of Bala Lake, Llanuwchllyn, and on a clear day as far as Cadair Idris to the west, open up.* Continue in a straight line and as you descend the hill you will come to a fence with a stile. Cross the stile and continue to walk downhill to the left, heading for the disused farm of Bwlch-y-fwlet.

**4** As you reach the fence above the farm turn right along the bottom of the field keeping the fence on your left. The path skirts around the hill and passes through

# Bala Lake Railway

two metal gates. After the second gate the fence falls away to your left and you continue straight across the field. At the end of the field cross a wooden stile and head across the next field to go through an open gap in the fence, and then head left down the field towards Bryncocyn farm. At the waymark sign head right to go

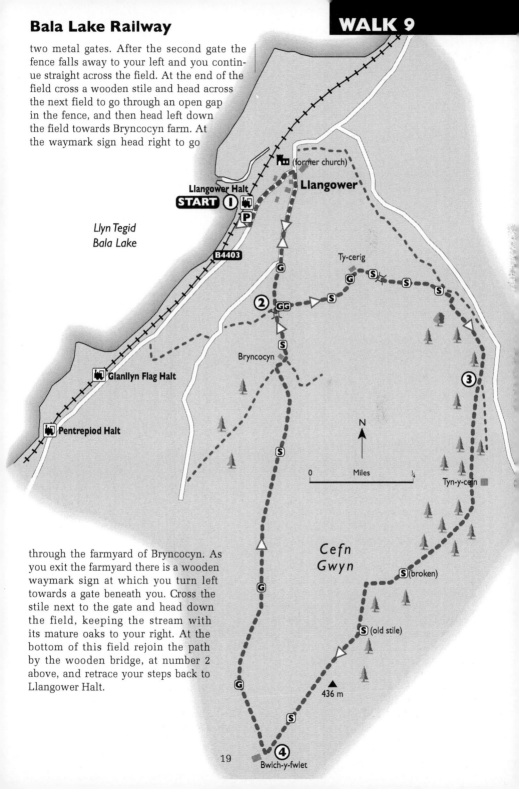

*Llyn Tegid*
*Bala Lake*

**START**

Llangower Halt

(former church)

**Llangower**

Ty-cerig

**2**

Bryncocyn

**3**

Glanllyn Flag Halt

Pentrepiod Halt

*Cefn Gwyn*

Tyn-y-cefn

S (broken)

S (old stile)

N

0    Miles    ¼

436 m

S

**4**
Bwlch-y-fwlet

through the farmyard of Bryncocyn. As you exit the farmyard there is a wooden waymark sign at which you turn left towards a gate beneath you. Cross the stile next to the gate and head down the field, keeping the stream with its mature oaks to your right. At the bottom of this field rejoin the path by the wooden bridge, at number 2 above, and retrace your steps back to Llangower Halt.

19

# WALK 10
# FEGLA FAWR

**DESCRIPTION** A gentle, mostly flat walk around the beautiful Fegla Fawr from Barmouth Ferry Station on the Fairbourne Railway, returning along the Mawddach Trail. This walk affords lovely views from Fegla Fawr across the estuary towards Barmouth, and up the estuary towards Dolgellau. 5 miles, 2½ hours round trip.
**START** From Barmouth Ferry station on the Fairbourne Railway, which is accessible from the railway or by ferry from Barmouth. There is also a small car parking area 400 yards south of the station which is an alternative start point for the walk, at Estuary Halt on the Fairbourne Railway.

**1** Take the path heading back south to the left of the railway track, away from the station. *As you walk take the opportunity to climb the dunes to your right to take in the view out to sea.* After 400 yards you come to the small car park which is the alternative starting point for the walk. Follow the road and at the Ardel Handen Recreation Park sign, bear left to cut off the corner of the road. As you rejoin the railway track and the road again at Loop Halt, turn sharp left at the footpath sign and head across an embankment up the valley.

**2** Walk along the embankment, built to contain the highest spring tides in the estuary, and enjoy views of Cader Idris, Barmouth and Fairbourne. On the hillside to your right are the old slate quarries, in which the Blue Lake is to be found. Pass through three wooden kissing gates, and then past an impressive rocky outcrop to your right, followed by a fourth kissing gate. At the end of the embankment, through another wooden kissing gate, there is a footpath sign. Turn right along the path next to the railway track. Cross the track through two metal gates and turn left along a tarmac path. After 20 yards turn right off the tarmac path at the footpath sign through another metal gate. Continue along this embankment until you reach the bottom of the hill, which is Fegla Fawr.

**3** Climb up the track and turn to the left, following the track curving gently left then right between the gorse bushes towards the top of the hill. *The path around Fegla Fawr affords lovely views back across the estuary towards the famous Barmouth Bridge, built in 1867 as Barmouth became a popular Victorian tourist destination.* As you progress round Fegla Fawr the path climbs into a beautiful secluded valley of oak trees, stunted by the sea winds. Descend to the bottom of the hill and turn right at the green footpath sign, around the back of the Victorian terraced houses of Mawddach

Pass through an old metal gate and walk past fields on your left, and old deciduous woodland to your right. At a wooden gate you reach the Mawddach Trail which traces the old railway line on the southern side of the estuary from Dolgellau to Fairborne and across the bridge to Barmouth.

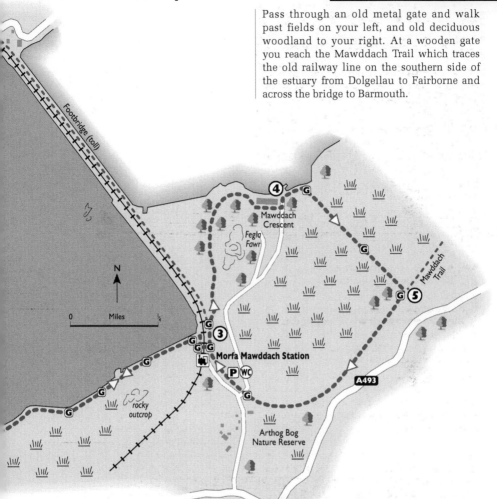

Crescent – *built in 1902 as part of a plan to build a tourist resort, with stunning views up the Mawddach estuary.*

**4** Past the houses turn left on to a minor tarmacked road and follow the road as it bears right past the beach. You can cool your feet in the water here, but take care for the dangerous currents in the estuary. Just before the cattle grid turn right through a gate at a footpath sign, and take the bridle path that leads off at a right angle to the road across the edge of an old oak wood, ignoring the path which runs next to the road.

**5** Turn right on the Trail in the direction of Fairbourne and Barmouth. The Trail passes through mature deciduous woodland and is also a well-used bike path. Pass the Arthog Bog nature reserve on your left, and go through a metal gate as a minor road comes in from the left and continue to follow the trail. Pass the public conveniences on your right and follow the path to Morfa Mawddach station. At the station turn left to cross back over the mainline railway taking care to look out for trains, and retrace your steps back along the embankment to your starting point.

# THE BLUE LAKE

**DESCRIPTION** A moderate short walk to the beautiful Blue Lake, hidden away in the disused quarry above Friog, with stunning views along the way over Fairbourne, Barmouth and the Mawddach Estuary. 2½ miles, 2 hours round trip.

**START** From the Fairbourne Steam Railway station in Fairbourne. There is parking along the roads close to the station.

**1** Turn right out of Fairbourne Steam Railway station and cross the mainline railway track. Take care to watch out for trains! Follow the road as it turns left past St Cynon's Church. At the junction with the A493 turn right towards Tywyn and enter the village of Friog. *Above on your left you will see the tailings of the disused slate mine in which the Blue Lake nestles.*

**2** After 325 yards turn left opposite a phone box into Fordd Panteinion. Follow the road as it rises gently up the hillside, with a stream to your right. Ignore a gate leading into the old quarry, and follow the road across a small bridge where the stream reappears on your left.

**3** At the footpath sign turn right, through a kissing gate, and follow the track as it begins to climb steeply. *As you emerge above the trees views of the sea begin to appear to your right. You will see the invasion defences built across the beach in the 1940s which are now the best preserved in Wales.* As the track curves left, turn right onto the path as it slopes up under a slate bridge. Take care as this is very slippery when wet. Continue to follow the path as it goes through the mine workings. Follow the path as it bears left through an archway under an old incline.

**4** Continue on under one more archway, and then turn immediately left to climb the short bank on to the top of the mine workings. *In good weather you will have stunning views over Fairbourne, Barmouth and the Mawddach Estuary. On this level you will see some of the abandoned mine machinery.* Keep the clump of conifers to your right, and just after the conifers enter the short tunnel to your right. Take care as the tunnel ceiling is low and wet and there are still some old railway tracks in the tunnel. Some of the water from the lake flows out through the tunnel. There are stepping stones to keep your feet dry as you creep through.

**5** As you emerge from the tunnel you are at the Blue Lake itself. *The lake is 46 feet deep and takes its colour from the slate and the reflections of the sky. It's a magical place for a picnic and there is an excellent echo!* Retrace your steps to return to Fairbourne Steam Railway station.

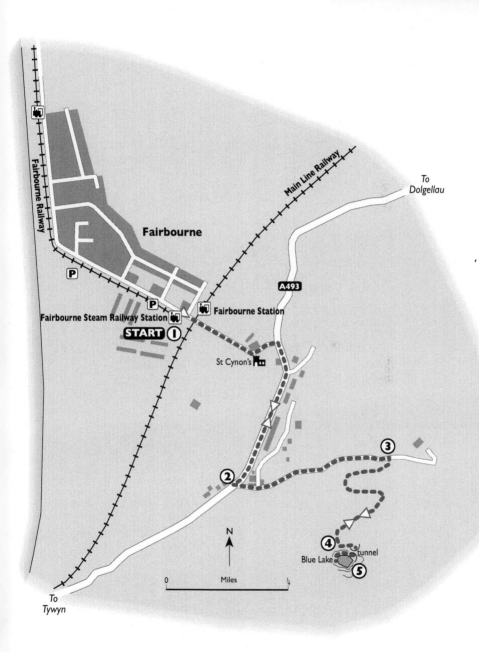

Fairbourne Railway

P

Main Line Railway

To
Dolgellau

Fairbourne

A493

P

P

Fairbourne Steam Railway Station

Fairbourne Station

START ①

St Cynon's

②

③

N

④ tunnel

Blue Lake

⑤

0    Miles    ¼

To
Tywyn

# THE HILLS ABOVE BARMOUTH

**DESCRIPTION** A ferry ride from Barmouth Ferry Station on the Fairbourne Railway and a moderate short walk above Barmouth, giving beautiful views over Barmouth and the Mawddach estuary, discovering a few hidden gems. 30 minutes for the ferry ride to and from Barmouth, and 2 hours, 2 miles walking.

**START** From Barmouth Ferry Station on the Fairbourne Railway. An alternative start point is the pay and display car park at the beach in Barmouth.

**I** Leave the station and walk straight to the ferry landing. The ferries run regularly during the summer season. Call Emily's Ferries on 07765 502404 to check times if you need to be sure. The ferry lands at the harbour in Barmouth.

**2** Leave the ferry and walk right towards the A496 and under the mainline railway. There are public conveniences on the promenade close to the ferry landing. (If you have started from the alternative car park start point, turn left from the car park and follow the road round to the left, then under the mainline railway.) At the A496 turn right, heading out of town, past The Last Inn and then Birmingham Garage on your left.

**3** As the road bears right, follow the signposted footpath left, and climb up the steep steps. At the top of the steps turn left through a metal gate and follow the path up the hillside. Shortly you come to a valley leading down to the town. Turn right and continue to follow the path up the hill. *Behind you there are lovely views of Barmouth, Fairbourne and the Mawddach estuary, and of your start point at Barmouth Ferry.* As the path climbs through the valley it passes through a small oak woodland. Go through a metal gate and the path becomes a grassy track, passing alongside a dry stone wall to the right. At a metal gate to your right take a sharp left and double back up the hillside, to see more beautiful views of the estuary and the Barmouth Railway Bridge.

**4** After a few yards, at a green waymark turn sharp right to double back on yourself again and continue along the hillside. There is a wooden bench here for a short rest and to enjoy the view over the estuary. Go through a metal gate into a field and follow the path left. After a few yards, where the path divides, follow the left hand fork, following the dry stone wall on your left up the hillside. The path then strikes right, away from the wall, skirting to the right around the foot of the hill. The path continues through a metal gate in a stone wall and past a fenced off mine entrance to your right. It continues through another metal gate, with a sheer rock face rising to the left, a training ground for early stage rock climbers. *Beautiful views can be seen to the right up the Mawddach estuary towards Dolgellau.*

**5** At a minor metalled road bear left. The road takes you over a ladder stile – *and into an exquisite hidden valley, overlooked by Gell-fawr.* Past the house follow the footpath sign left, and then left again, keeping the barbed wire fence to your left. Go through a metal gate with a waymark sign, over a small stream and then bear right to a waymark sign. At the waymark turn left up the hillside keeping the dry stone wall on your right. *Over the brow of the hill views of Fairbourne open up in front of you.* Just beyond the brow of the hill turn right and cross the dry stone wall at a stone stile, ignoring the gate ahead of you. As you come down the hill to a path, bear left towards Barmouth, past the beautiful ruins of the farm at Cell-fechan. Ignore the footpath going right towards Craig y Gigfran and continue straight down, through a metal gate. *Suddenly there are views over the streets of Barmouth below you.* Follow the path as it zigzags down the hillside, passing a number of old mine entrances, and through a metal gate above the church. Ignore the little path leading down to the left and the path brings you out on a minor metalled road. Turn left and follow this road as it takes you down St Johns Hill towards the High Street.

**6** On the High Street (A496) turn left, and then turn right to go across the mainline railway crossing and towards the beach. At the promenade turn left to return, past the alternative car park starting point, to the ferry landing. *There are plenty of places to buy lunch and an ice cream in Barmouth.*

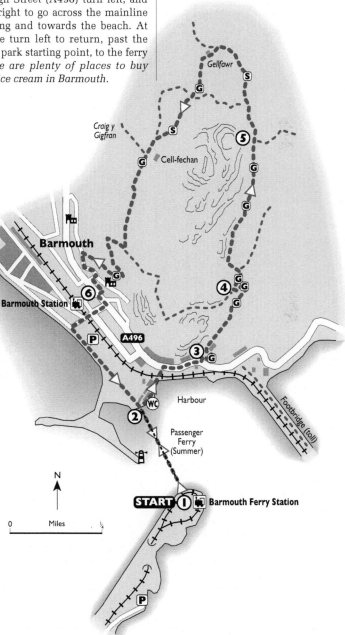

## WALK 13

# BIRDS' ROCK

**DESCRIPTION** A walk from Dolgoch Falls station on the Talyllyn railway around Birds' Rock, with stunning views of the beautiful Fathew and Dysinni valleys, and the Cadair Idris range. 4 hours, 5½ miles. Moderate.

**START** From Dolgoch Falls station on the Talyllyn Railway. The station car park is an alternative starting point for the walk.

**1** From Dolgoch Falls Station walk down to the car park and then walk 150 yards left along the road towards Tywyn to a green footpath sign on your right.

**2** Climb the stone steps, cross the stile and turn immediately right. Go through the metal gate and bear diagonally left up the hill heading for a small wood and another metal gate. Through the gate head along the grassy track and cross a ladder stile over a fence. Pass through another metal gate and around the back of Tan-y-coed-isaf. Go through another gate into the parking area of the house. From the parking area of the house head left at the green waymark past a small corrugated iron shed and through another metal gate. Continue along the grassy path as it rises a little away from the fence, and then cross a stile over a fence at a green waymark. *Ahead you see beautiful views up the Fathew Valley with the Talyllyn railway on your right.* Pass through another metal gate with a waymark, and at the next waymark ahead of you follow the path behind Tan-y-coed-uchaf. Behind the farm the path climbs steeply up the hillside through another metal gate, and then a wooden gate. Ignore another waymarked track that crosses from left to right, and carry straight on, gaining height sharply through an oak wood.

**3** As you exit the wood turn left on a metalled track past Rhiwerfa. *You will see views to your right of Mynydd Pennant, and the Cadir Idris range on the far side of the Dyffryn Dysinni.* Follow the track gently downwards and left and through a wooden gate, ignore Gelli-ddraenen to your right

and continue through another metal gate. At a waymark turn right off the metalled track downhill along a grassy track with hawthorns on your right. *There are beautiful views of the valley to your right.* Cross the stile to the left of a metal gate, and bear right across the field to a ladder stile and waymark. *In the far distance to the right you will see Cadair Idris.* Over the ladder stile bear right, heading down a faint track towards a metal gate, and then follow the grassy track as it curves left around the hillside and to another metal gate. *There is, for the adventurous, a path here that leads steeply up left to the top of Birds' Rock.* Continue to follow the grassy track gently, and then more steeply, downhill, keeping the dry stone wall on your right, to the road.

**4** Cross the stile and turn left on the road. *As you round the corner you will have an impressive view up towards Birds' Rock on your left. Birds' Rock is an outcrop of 840 feet, renowned as a cormorant nesting site even though the sea is now 6 miles away from the Rock!* Pass Wern farm on your right and at the road junction bear left signposted Bryn Crug. Follow the road around the base of Birds' Rock past Ty-coch farm on your left.

**5** After Gesail farm, take one last look behind you at Birds' Rock, and cross the stile at the footpath sign on the left and follow the path uphill. Cross the next stile and bear right up the hill through some broad-leaved bluebell woods, of oak and birch. Continue to bear right up the hillside, ignoring a small path which leads away to the right. Continue climbing past two more waymark signs. Exit the wood at a waymarked stile, bear right to skirt around the trees, and head for a fence and waymark post ahead of you to your right. Cross the stile and follow the path keeping close to the fence on your right. The track now passes a tumbledown building on the left. Continue straight ahead, past a path to the right and a waymark sign to your left. As the track curves left follow the fence to your right to the waymark sign and stile in the corner of the field to your right. Head across the next field, to the left of the trees ahead of you, and then head for the gate behind the brow of the hill ahead of you. Go through the gate and to the next gate, ahead to your right in the bottom corner

From this waymarker you will see a stile and the next waymarker on the left of a big oak tree. Cross the stile and head across the field a little to your right, heading for another oak tree. The path curves down and round to the right. Past the oak tree head down the field keeping close to the fence on your right. *As you head down the hill you will see the little valley of Nant Dolgoch ahead of you, with Bryn Crug and Mynydd Tan-y-coed on either side.*

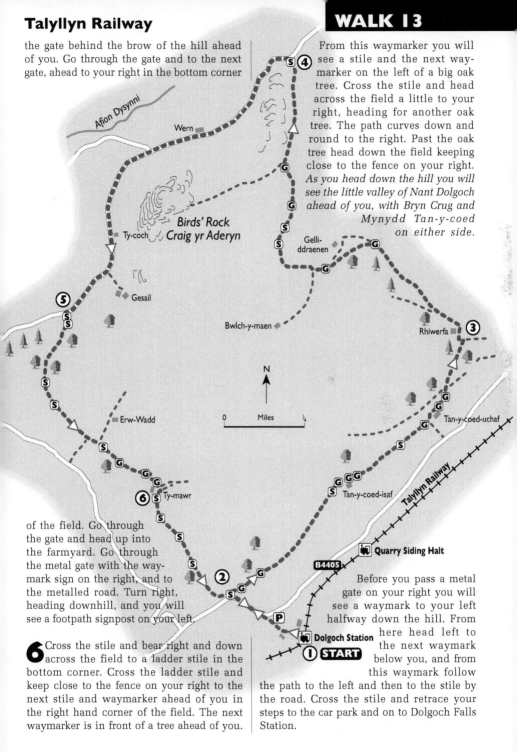

of the field. Go through the gate and head up into the farmyard. Go through the metal gate with the waymark sign on the right, and to the metalled road. Turn right, heading downhill, and you will see a footpath signpost on your left.

**6** Cross the stile and bear right and down across the field to a ladder stile in the bottom corner. Cross the ladder stile and keep close to the fence on your right to the next stile and waymarker ahead of you in the right hand corner of the field. The next waymarker is in front of a tree ahead of you.

Before you pass a metal gate on your right you will see a waymark to your left halfway down the hill. From here head left to the next waymark below you, and from this waymark follow the path to the left and then to the stile by the road. Cross the stile and retrace your steps to the car park and on to Dolgoch Falls Station.

# CASTELL Y BERE

**DESCRIPTION** A moderate and varied walk from Nant Gwernol station on the Talyllyn Railway to the stunning and mysterious Castell y Bere in the Dysynni valley, tracing some of the barefoot walk taken by Mary Jones in 1800. 5½ miles, 4 hours round trip.

**START** From Nant Gwernol station on the Talyllyn Railway. An alternative start point is the car park in the centre of Abergynolwyn village, opposite the Railway Inn.

**I** Leave Nant Gwernol station by the path at the far end of the platform. Keep left and ignore the steps going up the hill. Follow the path over the bridge and keep the stream with its waterfalls on your left. *There are pools here deep enough to bathe in the summer.* At the tarmac road turn left towards Abergynolwyn. *At the main road, B4405, there is a car park which is an alternative start point for the walk, and public conveniences. Abergynolwyn Village was founded in the 1860s for workers at the Bryn Eglwys quarry above Nant Gwernol.* Cross the main road with care and follow the road to the right of the Railway Inn. Follow this road up the hill which rises at first gently and then more steeply. Above the village ignore the minor road on your right and as you crest the hill look for a stile with a footpath sign on the right.

**2** Cross the stile and take the footpath diagonally up the hillside aiming for the waymark on the brow of the hill ahead, and then to a second waymark ahead of you. *There are beautiful and wide reaching views of the Dysynni Valley here.* Ignore a track which heads up to the right and continue straight on to the next waymark post tucked behind a clump of trees. Follow the direction indicated, sloping gently down and look for a waymarked wood and slate stile on your right. Cross the stile, and a small stream, and continue along, keeping the wall on your left. Go through the waymarked gate, ignore the gate ahead of you, and cross the stile immediately to your left. Head diagonally down

the hill to find a green track and head right on the green track looking for a kissing gate on the left between two old oaks. Go through the kissing gate and head half right down the hill towards a waymarked stile by the road. Cross the stile and head right on the road. *On your left is the entrance to Castell y Bere, built in 1221 by Llewellyn the Great to defend Gwynedd. The English took the castle in 1282, and it was besieged and burnt by Madoc ap Llewellyn in 1294. The castle is in ruins and is one of the most beautiful and peaceful spots in mid-Wales for a picnic.*

**3** Carry on past Castell y Bere, down the hill to the church at Llanfihangel-y-pennant. *This was the church attended by Mary Jones who in 1800 famously walked barefoot all the way from her house near the church to Bala to buy a Welsh language bible thereby inspiring the formation of the Bible Society.* Opposite the church follow the way-marked track on the right, past public conveniences on the right (not open year round). Follow the track and cross a ladder stile by a dilapidated chapel on the right and continue up the hill next to the stream past some small waterfalls. Take great care here as the rocks are very slippery in wet weather. The going is damp and boggy. Cross a stile and ignore a path and stile to the right and continue ahead. You will join a green track at a gate. Cross the ladder stile next to the gate and continue with the stream some way away on your right. Follow the track past the ruins of Nant-yr-eira and cross a small stream to a ladder stile by a gate. Cross the stile and follow the track. When you come to a wall on your right, bear right a little to reach a ladder stile by a sheepfold.

**4** Cross the stile and follow the path round to the left and you will see lovely views across the valley and of Graig Wen ahead. Follow the path as it goes down the hill and look for a waymarked path to the right. Turn right, down through the wood of small oaks and follow the waymark round to the left. Follow the path down to the ladder stile and gate in the bottom left hand corner of the field by the road junction.

**5** Cross the ladder stile by the gate and turn immediately right on the minor road. Walk along the road as it rises gently uphill, past Cedris Farm and Mariafel Ganol on your left. As you pass another house on the left you will see a clearly waymarked path on your left. Take this path down the well-

defined steps, and across a wooden stile. A few yards later cross another wooden stile, and then straight ahead of you cross a third stile and turn immediately right. Cross one more stile and walk along with the river to your left. Rejoin the road at a kissing gate by a bridge, and turn left to retrace your steps past the Railway Inn and up to Nant Gwernol station.

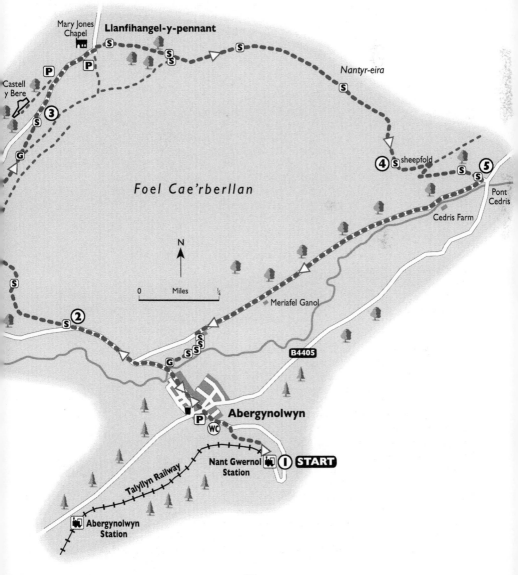

# NANT BRIACH-Y-RHIW

**DESCRIPTION** A gentle walk from Rhyd-yr-onen station on the Talyllyn Railway up the valley next to Nant Briach-y-rhiw and back. 2¼ miles, 1½ hours.

**START** From Rhyd-yr-onen station on the Talyllyn Railway.

**1** From the station platform walk to the road, and turn right over the bridge back over the railway. As the road turns left go straight on up a tarmac track and through a metal gate following the footpath signs. Follow the track up the hill. Where the track divides follow the left hand fork to a metal gate, and at the next gate follow the waymark through the right hand gate. At Briach-y-rhiw farm you will see the next waymark on a telegraph pole, pointing left through the farmyard. Go through the gate, and left through the farm yard. Bear right through the first gate, up the hill a few yards and then through the next gate. You will see the path ahead of you, climbing the hill side. Keep to the fence on your left and when the track forks again keep left.

**2** On your left you will see an underground reservoir. Continue climbing gently, passing through gates, towards coniferous woodland on your left, where you will see a pretty vista of stream and valley below to your left. *As you pass by the woodland look for the shady glades next to the stream through the trees below you.* The path exits the woods at a sheepfold with a metal gate. Pass through the gate up the valley, and after 50 yards bear left towards the stream and you will see a small concrete bridge ahead of you. Cross the bridge and bear gently left up the hillside until the path meets a minor metalled road.

**3** Turn sharp left on the road and follow it back down the valley, passing through a metal gate. *If you look up to the left you will see a disused quarry and workings above you.* Follow the road back down the valley to Rhyd-yr-onen station.

# Talyllyn Railway

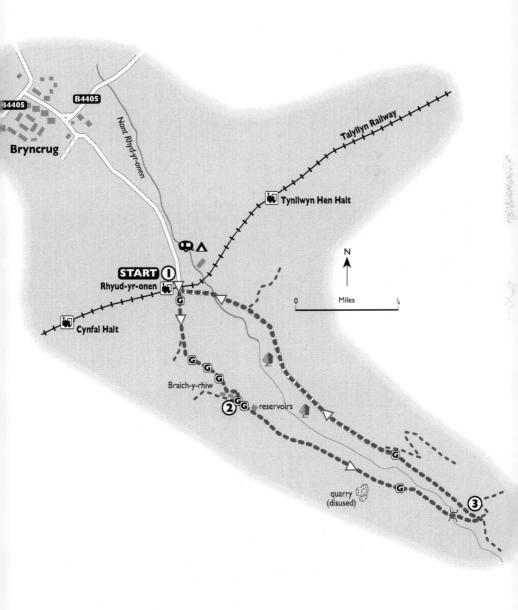

B4405

B4405

Bryncrug

Nant Rhyd-yr-onen

Talyllyn Railway

Tynllwyn Hen Halt

N

0    Miles    ¼

START ①
Rhyud-yr-onen

G

Cynfal Halt

G G
G
Braich-y-rhiw
② G G    reservoirs

G

G
quarry
(disused)    ③

31

# THE SUNKEN BRIDLEWAY ABOVE LLANFAIR CAEREINION

**DESCRIPTION** A gentle walk from Llanfair Caereinion Station on the Welshpool & Llanfair Railway through the town and up on top of the hill behind the town, going through a beautiful old sunken bridleway. 2 hours, 3 miles. Some moderate uphill walking.

**START** From Llanfair Caereinion Station on the Welshpool & Llanfair Railway. There is ample car parking available behind the station

**1** Exit the station away from the main road, towards the wooden footbridge over the Afon Banwy. Cross the footbridge and follow the path right into the town, following the blue signs for the town centre. Go down the steps towards the B4389, also called Bridge Street. Turn left for a few yards to the junction with Broad Street, and at the HSBC bank building turn sharp left up the B4385, Mount Road, passing the Spar shop on your right. Climb up the road, and turn left at the green footpath sign just past the recreation ground. Pass through a metal gate and head diagonally up the field to the far right hand corner. Cross the wooden fence and bear right across a few yards of wasteland then up a green track to a minor road, Peartree Lane.

**2** Bear left on Peartree Lane, passing Peartree farm on the left. The minor road becomes a grassy track and then a bridleway. Follow the bridleway right at a gate and across a wooden stile. Ahead of you up the hill is another bridleway sign and follow the sign, bearing left. *Soon you reach the highest point of this short walk, at 750 feet above sea level. From here there are panoramic views to the West over Llanfair Caereinion and the valleys, and to the East across the rolling hills towards Welshpool. The lush grass and gentle hills make for ideal sheep farming country.* Cross two wooden stiles and follow the ridge gently downhill ahead of you. *As you descend the ridge there are beautiful views of the valley and over the railway running between the trees on the valley floor. The bridleway you are following is fringed by old hawthorn hedges, and gradually sinks further beneath the hedgerow level. You are walking a very ancient route which has been used for hundreds of years across these hills. As you walk the bridleway, at some times 10 feet or so deep below the surrounding hedgerows, you will feel that time has stood still for centuries.* Cross another wooden stile.

**Llanfair Caereinion**

B4385

**3** At the bottom of the bridleway cross a wooden stile and turn left on the minor road, across a cattle grid and past Eithnog Farm on your right. The road dips and you cross another cattle grid. Then the road winds its way through the tiny, sleepy hamlet of Eithinog and past Eithinog Hall. Soon the Afon Banwy becomes audible and visible again to your right. As you come into the town again, turn right onto a minor road, Glanyrafon, and then turn right again at the blue signpost towards the station. Rejoin the path that takes you back across the wooden footbridge and back to the station.

# Welshpool & Llanfair Railway

Eithinog Farm

③

S

S

S

Welshpool & Llanfair Light Railway

Afon Banwy

Eithinog

A458

N

0    Miles    ¼

S

🏠 P ① START

S

S

Peartree

② ▽

G

B4385

# WALK 17
# THE MONTGOMERY CANAL

**DESCRIPTION** An easy walk from Raven Square Station in Welshpool on the Welshpool & Llanfair Railway through Welshpool, up the Montgomery Canal and back past Powis Castle. 3 hours, 5 miles.

**START** From Raven Square Station in Welshpool on the Welshpool & Llanfair Light Railway at Welshpool. An alternative start point is the public car park on Berriew Street in Welshpool.

**1** Turn right out of Welshpool Station, alongside the A458, into the centre of Welshpool. *This is an ideal time to buy something for lunch from one of the many bakeries on the High Street. Welshpool is an historic town which became a Borough in 1263. As you walk down the High Street notice the Town Hall on the left, which was built in 1810 and houses the old court-room, council chamber and assembly room.* Continue straight ahead at the crossroads by the Royal Oak onto Severn Street (B4381). To the right is Berriew Street, 100 yards along which there is a public car park which is an alternative start point for the walk, and public conveniences.

**2** At the bridge crossing over the Montgomery Canal turn right to join the Severn Way which runs along the tow-path on the left of the canal. Follow the path as it crosses under the main road, and then past the very pretty Belan Locks. *As you approach the locks the canal becomes increasingly peaceful as it travels through open countryside and you will see many different birds flying ahead of you. The Montgomery Canal was originally planned to transport lime for agricultural purposes, to improve the farmland of the Upper Severn Valley. The canal was started in 1794 and finally completed in 1821. It was profitable until the First World War, but between*

*the World Wars it became unprofitable, and was abandoned in 1944, following a breach at Perry Aqueduct in 1936. Since 1969 it has been been progressively restored and declared a Site of Special Scientific Interest due to the flourishing wildlife it supports.*

**3** At the next bridge, Sweeps Bridge, numbered 122, go under the bridge and through the wooden gate on the left, and turn left onto the minor road which takes you back and over the canal. Across the bridge turn immediately right through a metal gate, marked with a wooden waymark, doubling back on yourself with the canal now on your right. The path crosses a small stream and then climbs steadily up through mature deciduous woods to a wooden stile. Cross the stile and the track beyond it, and take the path opposite as it continues to climb to the right, up and out of the woods. As it leaves the wood the path keeps the woods close to the right, and then bears left across the field to a metal gate in the hedge. *As you cross the field views over the Severn Valley, and over Welshpool with its sheltering hills, open up. For thousands of years the Severn Valley was the main travelling and trade route between North and South Wales. The hedges and woodland here are old, and full of wildlife.* Go through the metal gate and continue straight ahead, keeping close to the hedge on your left. Cross a wooden stile from which you can see the Belan Locks below to your right. The path then descends through the field to join a small stream. At a wooden footpath sign cross the wooden stile and turn immediately left on a track through a metal gate and across an impressive stone bridge. Follow the track as it bears up and to the right, keeping the woodlands to your left. *This track links Powis Castle, which is over the hill ahead of you, and the Belan Locks. Many years ago the Castle estate would have been received many of its supplies along this track.*

**4** The track ends at a minor metalled road opposite the entrance to Powis Castle. *The Castle, originally built in 1200, has world-famous gardens, overhung with enormous clipped yews, and is now owned by*

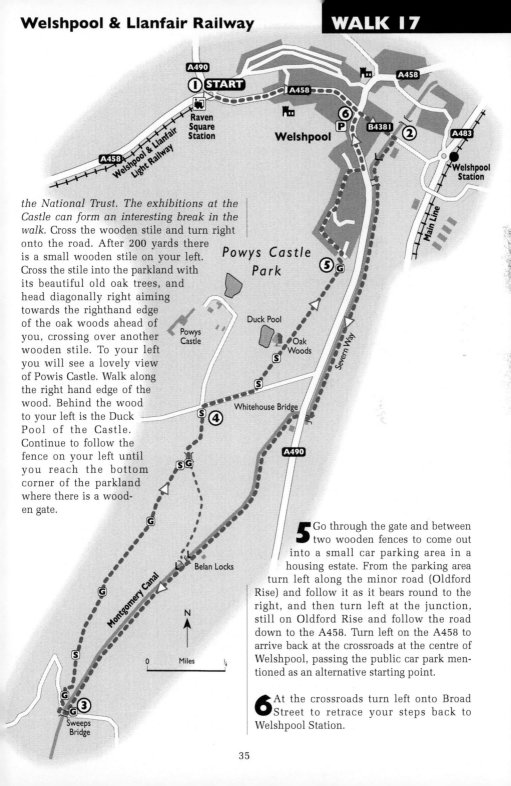

the National Trust. *The exhibitions at the Castle can form an interesting break in the walk.* Cross the wooden stile and turn right onto the road. After 200 yards there is a small wooden stile on your left. Cross the stile into the parkland with its beautiful old oak trees, and head diagonally right aiming towards the righthand edge of the oak woods ahead of you, crossing over another wooden stile. To your left you will see a lovely view of Powis Castle. Walk along the right hand edge of the wood. Behind the wood to your left is the Duck Pool of the Castle. Continue to follow the fence on your left until you reach the bottom corner of the parkland where there is a wooden gate.

**5** Go through the gate and between two wooden fences to come out into a small car parking area in a housing estate. From the parking area turn left along the minor road (Oldford Rise) and follow it as it bears round to the right, and then turn left at the junction, still on Oldford Rise and follow the road down to the A458. Turn left on the A458 to arrive back at the crossroads at the centre of Welshpool, passing the public car park mentioned as an alternative starting point.

**6** At the crossroads turn left onto Broad Street to retrace your steps back to Welshpool Station.

35

# ABERYSTWYTH CASTLE, CLIFF RAILWAY & PENGLAIS FACH

**DESCRIPTION** A moderate walk from Aberystwyth Station on the Vale of Rheidol railway past the harbour and castle, along the front, up Constitution Hill and over Penglais Fach and around the golf course. 3 hours, 4 miles.

**START** At Aberystwyth Station on the Vale of Rheidol railway. An alternative start point is the public car park on Park Avenue next to the Station. There are public conveniences opposite the car park.

**1** From Aberystwyth Station follow walk number 19 past the Harbour, Castle and Promenade and up to the top of Constitution Hill.

**2** At the top of the hill, after a short rest and an ice cream, go back on to the path and ignore the Welsh Coastal path to the left. Continue to follow our path, signposted to the right with a green waymark. Behind Constitution Hill follow the path left at a waymark through a gate and down a gravel track. Follow the track around the back of a radar station, eventually turning left next to the road leading to Ty-Hên. Behind Ty-Hên pass through a gate where the footpath has

been diverted, and then right through another gate, and finally through another gate and follow the gravelled track. As you pass the golf course on the right, follow the footpath right as it cuts off a corner of the track. Follow the track right again as it skirts the golf course and ignore both the minor road and the footpath on your left. Our track continues downhill through the golf course, so take care as you pass one of tees on your left.

**3** At the minor road turn right, and past the Aberystwyth Nurseries bear immediately left on a track through light woodland. After a few yards turn left again before a metal gate, through deciduous woodland with beautiful wild flowers fringing the path. The path becomes a minor road. Cross over Castell Brychan/Bryn Road and go down the metalled path opposite, marked Gelli Anwen. *This is named in memory of Anwen*

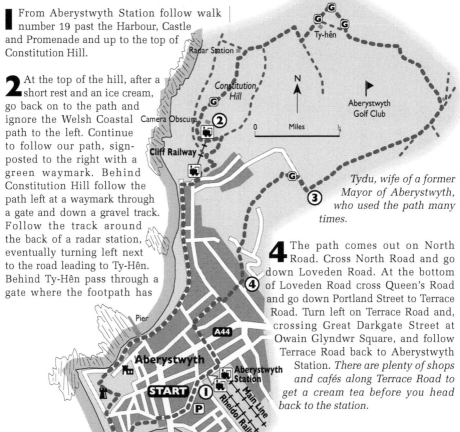

*Tydu, wife of a former Mayor of Aberystwyth, who used the path many times.*

**4** The path comes out on North Road. Cross North Road and go down Loveden Road. At the bottom of Loveden Road cross Queen's Road and go down Portland Street to Terrace Road. Turn left on Terrace Road and, crossing Great Darkgate Street at Owain Glyndwr Square, and follow Terrace Road back to Aberystwyth Station. *There are plenty of shops and cafés along Terrace Road to get a cream tea before you head back to the station.*

## WALK 19
# ABERYSTWYTH HARBOUR, CASTLE & CLIFF RAILWAY

**DESCRIPTION** A moderate walk from Aberystwyth Station on the Vale of Rheidol railway past the harbour and castle, along the Promenade and up Constitution Hill. 2 hours, 2½ miles.

**START** At Aberystwyth Station on the Vale of Rheidol railway. An alternative start point is the public car park on Park Avenue next to the Station. There are toilets opposite the car park.

**1** From the railway station walk towards the town and turn immediately left along Alexandra Road, outside the impressive main line station which was built in the 1920s. At the roundabout go straight across, along Mill Street using the pedestrian lights. (The public car park is 100 yards up Park Avenue – the left turn at this roundabout – on the right.) As the road turns left to cross the bridge, go straight on just to the right of Rummers Bar. Behind the bar descend the steps to the left and turn right at the bottom. Follow the road as it takes you around the old Harbour area. *In the 19th century passage was available direct to the New World from Aberystwyth Harbour.* Follow the road towards South Beach, and turn right on the New Promenade.

**2** At South Road bear right to the castle, and follow the path right, around the walls and then left as it turns into the castle itself. *The castle was built by the English between 1277 and 1289, was captured in 1404 by Owain Glyndŵr, but was recaptured again in 1408.* Walk through the circle of standing stones, erected for the 1916 Eisteddfod, and through the gateway ahead of you. As you exit the castle towards the War Memorial, turn right and descend the steps down to the New Promenade. Follow the New Promenade right, past the original buildings

of Aberystwyth University *founded in 1872,* past the Pier and past North Beach to your left. Ahead you will see Constitution Hill and the Cliff Railway.

**3** At the end of the New Promenade turn right up Cliff Terrace to the Cliff Railway Station. *The Cliff Railway was opened in 1896 as a tourist attraction.* Just to the right of the Station look for a wooden signpost for Constitution Hill and follow the path right as it climbs steeply behind the houses between gorse and blackberry bushes. When the path has doubled back to the Cliff Railway take the right hand fork back again, ignoring the bridge and the stone steps. *At the higher of the two bridges over the railway you are rewarded with a fabulous view back over Aberystwyth town, North Beach, the Pier and the Castle.* Cross the higher bridge towards the sea and follow the path as it bears right and upwards, to Constitution Hill.

**4** *Take time here to enjoy the views. There are cafés next to the Summit Terminus of the Cliff Railway for a well-earned cup of tea, or an ice cream.* Return down the hill along the Promenade and past the Castle and Harbour to your starting point.

37

## WALK 20

# THE VALE OF RHEIDOL

**DESCRIPTION** A walk from Devil's Bridge Station on the Vale of Rheidol Railway down into the valley of the Afon Rheidol and back. This moderate walk affords stunning views of the Vale of Rheidol and at the midpoint passes a picnic spot on the Afon Rheidol. The walk is for the most part gentle, with a couple of short steep climbs. A total of 600 feet is lost and then regained on the walk. 3 hours, 5 miles

**START** From Devil's Bridge Station on the Vale of Rheidol Railway. An alternative starting point is the free Waterfalls Car Park 200 yards down the A4120 from the station. Opposite the station there are also Public Conveniences open all year round.

**I** Turn right out of Devil's Bridge Station and follow the A4120 up for 300 yards. Immediately after the last house on the right turn right at the wooden footpath sign through a wooden gate onto the path from Devil's Bridge to Borth. *Borth is 18 miles away on the coast, but we will not go the whole way today!* Follow the wooden marker posts as the path descends into the valley to join the railway, then follow the waymarks as they take the path a little left, away from the railway, to cross Nant y Fawnog over a wooden footbridge. *Across the railway there are lovely views of the Vale of Rheidol.* The path continues through ancient broadleaved woodland, part of the only ancient woodland in North Ceredigion, and joins up again with the railway and allowing more views back up the valley towards the Mynach Falls.

**2** The path crosses the railway and descends sharply into a mature conifer forest. *The Vale of Rheidol Railway was originally conceived in 1897 to serve the lead mines in the Vale of Rheidol. The mines closed during the First World War, and the railway reverted to passenger services only. After the Second World War ownership of the railway eventually passed to British Rail and it became the last* *steam railway operated by British Rail. From 1968 until privatisation in 1989 it was British Rail's only steam railway. It is now owned by a charitable trust.* As you reach the bottom of the forest the sounds of the Afon Rheidol rise to meet you as you enter, and walk through, the Coed Rheidol National Nature Reserve.

**3** At the far end of the Nature Reserve there is a wooden gate with a stile. Ignore this and instead take a sharp left, doubling back on yourself, and climb sharply back up through the nature reserve. *Behind you views across the valley towards the disused lead mine open up. The lead mine is noticeable from the ochre coloured deposits, and 100 years ago was a major source of pollution through the valley and as far as the sea.* As you reach the edge of the wood, turn sharply right on a wide grassy path. The path descends and becomes flat and easy, with views across the peaceful flat green farmland of the Vale of Rheidol down towards Aberystwyth, with the steep hills rising up on either side. The path winds its way gently just above the valley floor, through mature broad leaved woodland, and crosses a small stream over a slate-built footbridge. *As you walk beside the gentle river it is difficult to*

38

*imagine the fierce falls 2 miles upstream, and the old industrial heritage of the valley.* At some disused mine workings follow the path through a gate and keep left to keep close to the fence on your left. Follow the path as it passes just below some old industrial workings. The footpath leaves the fence and heads across a green field towards a weir on the Afon Rheidol. Just to the left of the weir cross a wooden stile and follow the path between two fences to a small picnic area with views up the valley. *You are halfway round now, so take some time to rest and admire the waterfall on the river while you eat your picnic. There is a fish ladder here too.*

**4** Cross the green footbridge over the Afon Rheidol, and follow the path up to a minor metalled road. Turn sharp right on the road and walk along the road, back up the valley. Pass the Bethel Chapel on your left – *built in 1872 during the popular non-conformist Welsh Christian revival in the late 19th century.* Ignore the bridle path which fords the river to your right, and then turn right to cross the Afon Rheidol over a grass covered concrete bridge. *The river is still, dark and deep here.* Follow the path to the left as it climbs back up the valley and cross the wooden stile into Coed Rheidol National Nature Reserve. From here (number 3 on the map) retrace your steps along the left hand fork which takes you back up through the woodland (in the conifer wood take care to take the right fork as indicated by the waymark), across the railway and back to Devil's Bridge Station.

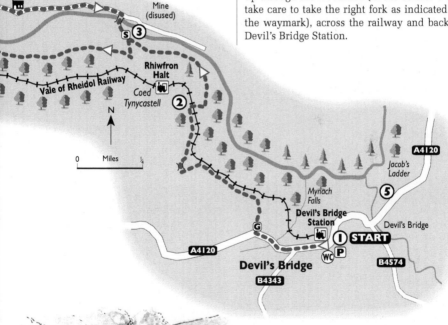

**5** If you have time when you arrive back at Devil's Bridge Station walk down the A4120 beyond the Station to the Waterfalls. *For a small fee you can walk down to view the three bridges and Jacob's Ladder on one side of the road, and the Devil's Punchbowl itself on the other.*

## PRONUNCIATION

| Welsh | English equivalent |
|---|---|
| c | always hard, as in **c**at |
| ch | as in the Scottish word lo**ch** |
| dd | as th in **th**en |
| f | as f in o**f** |
| ff | as ff in o**ff** |
| g | always hard as in **g**ot |
| ll | no real equivalent. It is like 'th' in then, but with an 'L' sound added to it, giving 'thlan' for the pronunciation of the Welsh 'Llan'. |

In Welsh the accent usually falls on the last-but-one syllable of a word.

## KEY TO THE MAPS

- ➤ Walk route and direction
- Metalled road
- - - Unsurfaced road
- •••• Footpath/route adjoining walk route
- ~~~➜ River/stream
- Trees
- Railway
- **G** Gate
- **S** Stile
- **F.B.** Footbridge
- Viewpoint
- P Parking
- T Telephone

## THE COUNTRYSIDE CODE

- Be safe – plan ahead and follow any signs
- Leave gates and property as you find them
- Protect plants and animals, and take your litter home
- Keep dogs under close control
- Consider other people

**David and Catherine Wightman** have been walking in Wales for most of their lives. David combines his love of walking with a love of steam railways, especially the Talyllyn, and Catherine combines her love of walking with a love of wildlife. They live part of each year above Bontddu and walk regularly in Wales.

Published by **Kittiwake-Books Limited**
3 Glantwymyn Village Workshops, Glantwymyn, Machynlleth, Montgomeryshire SY20 8LY
© Text & map research: David & Catherine Wightman 2013
© Maps & illustrations: Kittiwake 2013
*Drawings by* Morag Perrott
*Cover photos: Main* – Welsh Highland Railway. *Back cover, left to right* – Bala Lake Railway; Ffestiniog Railway; Welshpool & Llanfair Railway; Talyllyn Railway. David Perrott

Printed by MWL, Pontypool.

ISBN: **978 1 908 748 06 5**